CREEPY FANTASY
KAWAii PASTEL COLORING BOOK

this book belongs to

____

____

____

COLOR TEST

Dear beloved reader,

l hope this message finds you well, and that you are enjoying your time coloring through the pages of "Creepy Kawaii Gothic Pastel: Coloring Book Of Cute Horrors". As the author, l am grateful for your support and your choice to bring my designs to life with your creativity.

The inspiration behind this book came from a desire to blend two seemingly opposite themes, creating unique and captivating artwork that speaks to the heart. It is a celebration of cute and creepy, gothic and pastel, horror and joy, all carefully intertwined to create a mesmerizing experience for the senses.

l would like to kindly ask you to take a moment to share your thoughts on our Amazon page. Your feedback is essential to us as it helps us learn and improve our products to meet your needs better. We hope that you have enjoyed coloring in the 30 unique designs, and that this book has provided both entertainment and relaxation in equal measure.

Your review will also help other potential buyers make informed decisions about whether this book is right for them. Therefore, we kindly request that you share your honest feedback with us, so that we may continue to create content that resonates with our audience.

Once again, thank you for your support, and we look forward to hearing from you soon.

Warm regards,

Violet Dreamweaver